Along The Liffey
Poems and Short Stories

SHEILA O'HAGAN

salmonpoetry

Published in 2009 by
Salmon Poetry
Cliffs of Moher, County Clare, Ireland
Website: www.salmonpoetry.com
Email: info@salmonpoetry.com

Copyright © Sheila O'Hagan 2009

ISBN 978-1-907056-09-3

All rights reserved. No part of this publication may be reproduced or transmitted in any form or by any means, electronic or mechanical, including photography, recording, or any information storage or retrieval system, without permission in writing from the publisher. The book is sold subject to the condition that it shall not, by way of trade or otherwise, be lent, resold or otherwise circulated without the publisher's prior consent in any form of binding or cover other than that in which it is published and without a similar condition, including this condition, being imposed on the subsequent purchaser.

Cover artwork: Maura Harmon
Cover design & typesetting: Siobhán Hutson
Printed in England by imprint*digital*.net

Along The Liffey: Poems and Short Stories
receives financial assistance from the Arts Council

Acknowledgements

Acknowledgements are due to the following publications in which some of these poems and short stories were previously published:

The Adirondack Review, Atlanta Review, Berkeley Poetry Review, nth position, The Sunday Tribune, Syracuse Review, The Works & Working Papers in Irish Studies.

"Busaras Encounters" first appeared in *Salmon: A Journey in Poetry, 1981-2007*.

I also wish to thank Loyola Marymount University for a 2006 Summer Research Grant that allowed me to complete the book in a timely fashion.

Contents

Along The Liffey	11
Dusk Over Stephen's Green	12
The Dying Light	13
Advent of Spring	14
SHORT STORY: The Stars Are Shining	15
Elegy for Ted	22
Elegy for Mark	24
Talking to Whales	25
Grieving	26
The Sadness of the Dead	27
SHORT STORY: Dodo and I	29
The Angel of Mons	39
The Misjudgement of Paris	41
Theseus and Ariadne	42
Dido and Aeneas	43
Antigone	44
The Return of Odysseus to Ithaca	45
SHORT STORY: The Traveller	47
Vermeer's Milkmaid	55
Looking into Corot's 'Ville d'Avray'	56

Bonnard's Waterwoman	57
Painting Seamus Heaney	59
Lazarus To His Sisters	60
SHORT STORY: The Stag	61
Mirage	65
The Witching Hour	66
Night Air	67
Asphodel	68
The Wood Pigeon	69
Desecration	70
SHORT STORY: The Intruder	71

Along The Liffey

Houses upside down in water are not there.
If I step into the river, open doors,
No one will call out to me, or lean to talk
About the city flowing past, and if I walk

The watery streets no eyes will stare
For the dead can't see, each stricken flare
But a soul's last cry as it slips away
To the ambered caverns of the hard dark sea.

I pull my shade out of the water, cross the bridge,
Give back the river's cinema, its gold mirage
Hopeless to search drowned houses for your ghost.
What's left of love is warm beneath my coat.

Dusk Over Stephen's Green

Drawn to the event of dusk
I observe from my high window
Darkness loiter under trees
Shifting familiar shapes so leaves
Are chameleon, park rails
Black as thieves and my fine domain
Sinks into drowsy beds whose flowers
Bereft of their flame lie down
To await resurrection.

Now my eyes, seeking new forms
Readjust their conception of light
So those creatures I've yearned for
Since dawn begin to shape up
And I merge with the narratives of night
Share with the stars their glamorous lair
As Diana the Huntress lopes by
Trailing her fiery hair, those seven
Flighty Sisters in pursuit.

The Dying Light

Dusk falls, her persistent curtain
Closing on the day, fading the
Roofless blue that shepherds me
Yet night's cacophonies

And the moan of the moon
As she creaks up the waning sky
Lighting a surprise of violets
In the dusk, confirm that I am.

Soon moths and birds fly upside down
To tell the future. The day is undressed,
All is on trust. I close my eyes and sigh
For daylight's lovely visions to return.

Advent of Spring

This blackbird, little Wolfgang of the woods,
from the geometry of winter trees, pipes in
the entrance of the Spring, his yellow tip
Exuberant with thrills. A pale sun runs
its fingers through the streams, their rites
silvery, continuous. Underfoot the heft
of new shoots surging towards the light
fills my eyes with the newgreen sheen of spring.

Soon wood flowers will out like courtesans
wooed by the obstreperous young winds,
shop windows fill with fripperies, the faces
of the people change. Smiling like children
octogenarians will venture out, whilst you and I,
though neither young nor old, shout alleluia.

The Stars are Shining

At thirteen a promise is a promise, my father said to me. The Opera had come to town. 'Tosca's our man', he'd said. 'We'll climb to the Gods. Get the front row, one and sixpence. Just you and me, eh?'

It was a promise I took very seriously. My father was taking me to the Opera; we would sit in the Gods, the highest seats in the house, and the cheapest. A vision filled my eyes, of our heads touching the stars, our seats shining thrones from where we looked down on Tosca and the tragic Cavaradossi. And music ascending, transforming us into divine creatures. Would we not be the centre of the evening? The singers too, of course.

Every year the Opera came to our small city of Dublin. My father, his soul as full of music as any Dubliner's, turned out with the best of those who walked from Rathmines and Rathgar, Phibsboro and Ballymun, to hear Tosca, Traviata, La Bohéme. Through the dusk of autumn evenings when the city lit up too early for the afternoon's light, they hurried, chiaroscuro figures vanishing into halls and theatres. By seven thirty, the streets were empty. At ten thirty, when they poured out again, the streets seemed brighter, the city kinder.

That year, 1951, the host company was playing Tosca. My father idolised Puccini. The title role would be sung by the diva, Anna Palestrina. There was also to be the visiting tenor. 'E Lucevan Le Stelle'– 'The Stars are Shining'. What an aria! I knew his excitement was to do with the new Italian tenor, whom the more often he mentioned, the safer the promise.

The day came, and with it the usual problem. My father was fond of the bottle. As things were for him, he might stay in the house, he might go out. If he went out, it could be the last I'd see of him for the day, and the night too, maybe. I must do nothing to cross him until the hour set for departure. It would be up to me and I was very uneasy.

But there was little I could do, so I concentrated on the problem of what I should wear to the theatre. Anything to take my mind off the awful possibility of failure. One week before, I had ironed my best frock and hung it up where I could see it, a honey silk that slid through my hands like water. I studied my hair in the mirror. Would I wear it up in plaits around my head, or falling on my shoulders? And would he notice if I wore a little lipstick? I wondered what sort of people would be sitting in the Gods. Not the women in beautiful dresses they lifted above their knees to climb up the steps of the Dress Circle. Our seats might be the cheapest, I reassured myself, but not everyone got to sit with a wonderful man like my Dad who knew so much about music and the singers.

The day came. He was up early. I heard him below, banging the kettle on the stove, rattling cups, whistling to himself. A good start. I got down to the kitchen quickly to show appreciation. On the table, two fried eggs smiling up at me, a mug of tea freshly poured. He was already dressed, spruce as ever, hair slicked back, keeping himself busy, dish towel over his shoulder, hand on the frying pan.

'Opera tonight, Dad.'

No reply.

'Will I slip out for the paper?'

'I'll get my own paper, thanks.'

An edge to his voice? I was going wrong already, trying too hard maybe. At ten o'clock he reached for his coat to go out. I said nothing. If he'd picked his moment, anything you said would be misconstrued. 'It's started early', I thought in misery, all faith deserting me. But if my heart was leaden, my head still rang with his words:

'Ah, Tosca. Singing her heart out to Scarpia to save her man. All for nothing. Scarpia has him shot. And he singing to the stars – "E Lucevan Le Stelle". The whole soul of the man in that aria. Poor Cavaradossi! You don't need to know Italian, love. The music tells the story. No one can tell it like Puccini.'

An hour later, key in the hall door, he steps into the hall.

'Pattie, are you there?'

Was he wanting marks for being good?, I thought bitterly, unable to answer him. He hadn't been out to buy drink. I was sure of that. I knew his moods. The craving meant a dark look on his face, eyes avoiding you, a hand continually wiping the dryness of his mouth. I checked the paper bag he left on the table as he went to the bathroom. A paper, cigarettes, shoes he'd had soled and heeled. Not that he would have left the bag around if there was anything in it. So what had made him snap at me? Knowing the pressure was on him, I suppose.

Anyway, the mood was good now. It seemed set for the day. His shoes were polished with much spitting and rubbing, smell of boot black filling the kitchen. Best trousers were brought out and pressed with flicks of water and a hot iron. He sang around the house, little excerpts from Tosca, made endless cups of tea, went through his repetoire of silly jokes I'd heard many times before – 'Tell your mother thanks for the rabbit but the fish was a cod.' Or, 'If the sky fell, we'd catch larks!' It was the way he told them, lifting his eyebrows, giving a little whistle on the punch line. I laughed.

At three o'clock, he went out again. I stood on the steps, watching him go down the road. I hadn't dared to ask him where he was going. I knew he was restless, and I knew he was trying. Slowly, I looked at the day. The sun was shining. The house was bathed in the soft light from the sea, at the end of our road. My spirits lifted. I could see Tosca standing on the waves, singing of her love, and the black cloud of Scarpia moving across the waves. Oh, would he be good and not disappoint me? I took a deep breath, tried to feel trusting, went back inside the house.

He came home soon, a flush on his face from his walk by the sea. He was still humming little tunes. But he was watching the clock, unable to sit still. Opening time, I thought. I coaxed and petted him. 'Have a cup of tea with me', I said. 'I don't think this Tosca had a notion of how to save her man. Wouldn't she know Scarpia was not to be trusted?'

'Now, now, you don't know. Wait for the music to tell you', he said again. 'When Scarpia comes on stage, it gets loud and menacing. Listen for that, love.'

I'd engaged him. He talked. I listened, keeping his cup full, asking him questions I knew he'd love to answer, until it was time to get ready. At six o'clock, I came down the stairs, my gold frock swishing against the banisters, my hair falling around my shoulders, slightest touch of lipstick.

'You look grand, Pattie love. Off we go then. Your man is waiting for us.'

He couldn't stop mentioning the Italian tenor, whistling the arias, turning round in the street to look at something that amused him, raising his hat to all who passed, and drawing me into harmless jokes, his eyes full of humour. 'If the sky fell, we'd catch larks.' I caught his mood, swinging along with him, both of us giddy with expectation.

Outside the Gaiety, a queue had already formed but not too long, I thought, to stop us getting a good seat. The line lengthened. A busker walked up and down with a noisy ukulele. My father wise-cracked with him, and with the crowd. He nudged me, his eyes drawing mine to some coins on the ground, unclaimed.

'Watch this', he whispered. Putting his hand in his pocket, he pulled out some change, dropped a few pennies, bent to pick them up, scooping in the unnoticed silver. I laughed at his cleverness. 'Always keep your eyes on the ground, Pattie love', he said, winking at me to share conspiracy.

The doors opened. He got the tickets, thick orange ones, a shilling and sixpence each. We went through the entrance marked 'Upper Balconies', climbed up and up. He had to stop halfway to get his breath. But we still made it to the front row of the highest balcony, the Gods, as it was known, where we could lean over and watch the orchestra filing in, and he could indulge in a flow of remarks on the crowd below, the 'hoy paloy', as he called them, in the expensive seats near to the stage.

'Look at that Jemser, with his spats and tails, and his missus decked out like a bejewelled doughnut. And there's Alfie Byrne, down in the box with the Taoiseach. "Snap me now, Shakespeare", he'll be saying to Bill Shakespeare, who follows him around like a stray dog. And look at "The Dowager" with the Taoiseach.'

'Do stop, Dad', I said, laughing. But I was eager for more.

Alfie Byrne was the much-loved Lord Mayor of Dublin. Bill Shakespeare was his photographer who accompanied him on all his public obligations. And the lady whom Dad referred to as "The Dowager" was not the wife of the Taoiseach but the Taoiseach's mother who liked to be referred to as "The Dowager".

Now the orchestra had finished tuning up. The theatre went very quiet. The music began quietly, soared, grew calm, soared again, as the overture prepared me for the story of the tragic Tosca. My father had told me I would hear all the arias of the Opera in the overture. But I was unprepared for the shock when the curtain went up. The stage was gaudy. Tosca was fat. Cavaradossi, my father's wonderful tenor, was fat. Scarpia had a double chin, though that was alright as he was the villain.

But when the singing started, so did the magic. All the drama of the overture began to be played out, the artists strutting around the stage in their dazzling costumes, their faces contorted with the effort to sing above the wailing violins, the brass and woodwind. I looked at my father. He was transported, his eyes shining, his hands clutching each other on his lap. Perfumes from the best seats wafted up to mix with the sweat and heat of the gallery.

We sat through three acts. I too was transported, each aria bringing me to the brink of tears. The mood on the stage and in the theatre grew more and more taut, until I recognised in the pure sweetness of Cavaradossi's final plea the aria my father so loved. I leaned close to him, aware of his emotion, as if the power of the arias was sweeping him out of his own tragic frustrations. 'E lucevan le stelle', he murmured to himself – 'the stars are shining'. And his face softened into a dreamy fulfilment. The opera got tumultuous applause. Over and over, the artistes swept back onto the stage to take their bows. 'Good man yourself', my father shouted at the principal tenor. 'Good man yourself'. He caught my hand, squeezed it. Then turned to the man beside him. 'Wasn't that powerful now? Did you ever hear anything like it? Puccini's your man. None like him, eh? They did him well. They did him well.'

We reached the streets, giddy with the winding descent from such a height. The night was fine, not a cloud in the sky.

'Let's walk home, love', he said.

I walked beside him, along Dame Street, across O'Connell Bridge. The whole city was golden, the Liffey gleamed like shining foil. Trams passed us, full of flushed faces pressed to the windows. I wondered had the whole city been to the Opera. Slipping my hand through his arm, I linked us together, listening to his whistled tunes from the score, stepping jauntily with him through the streets up to Parnell Square. He turned to smile at an old man dancing, including me with a squeeze of his arm. 'E lucevan le stelle', he said, looking up at the sky, 'the stars are shining'.

★

Elegy for Ted

At four a.m. today my lover died
He didn't reach for me or call my name
Dreaming he would waken by my side
But turned his face and shuddered as some shame
Or haunting shook him and his mouth gave cry
To a portentous and unearthly pain.

Between darkness and dawn that cry of pain
And nothing warm has reached me since it died
Some ethos of cold starlight I can't name
Possessed my love while he lay by my side
Something strange, inhuman, born of shame
He had not said goodbye, called out, or cried

Some ghost or spirit left his mouth that cried
Out and he'd gone from me, had gone in pain
Into an alien world yet as he died
He drew my spirit to him, gave her my name
Something possessed him as he left my side
His face was turned away as though in shame

I took his absent face and murmured shame
To that which claimed him, for my love had cried
As though some shady trafficking in pain
Some curse or Judas kiss by which he died
Unknowingly in another's name
Had come to term as he lay down beside

The one he loved. Perhaps lying by his side
Fearful in sleep, I had called up that shame
And he, my love, unknowingly had cried
Out in redemption for another's pain
As though a chosen victim. My love died
Because some cursed spirit took his name.

For he was loved and honoured in his name
And I, as I lay sleeping by his side
Guarding his innocence, knew of no shame
On the stark cusp of dark and dawn he cried
Aloud so strange my heart burned cold with pain.
Not one warm thought has reached me since he died.

Still I call his name. All hope has died.
My unspent love's my pain. I have not cried.
Such is winter's shame, all's bare outside.

Elegy for Mark

In the stored past of an attic
I, a woman growing old
Hold a coat, Oxfam, with rabbit pin,
That shapes the lie of your presence,
Arrange the sleeves in an embrace
Search for a familiar hair or stain
Mourning as older women do
The bodies of the young.

Watch how your shade invades the pool
Of sun the window has let in
Hear the purr of the Silver Dream
Racer along a country road
See it turn treacherous
As you bend to the fatal spin
The reflection of your stillness
In the still-turning wheels.

I, a woman growing old
Perform a ritual for another's son
Loved as my own, rock myself
Into a grief black as the coat
I hold lest you be there, once a year
Climbing the height of this house
Far from any who might hear
The beat of the heart mending.

Talking to Whales

(Lament for Sile Beg)

Dear One, my finest memories of you
Are when I took the plane to San Diego
And we had two whole weeks of barbarous views
Across the desert and the Bay of San Francisco.

When we went to Mexico and both despised
In the border town we stopped at, tourists
Haggling as they cut the locals down to size
For a few pesos worth of nickels and dimes.

The ocean was the best. Going out to see
The whales. You loved their siren songs,
Their domesticity. I marvelled at the dolphins
Sparring with the boat, laughing with us, at us.

And on that day when you were feeling well,
We ventured out across the rocks. "Look, see",
You said, as you ran barefoot over them,
It was a miracle you put on for me.

But when we caught the desert's day of flowering
That brilliant carnival — did I sense your dust?
Was mine the inside eye that saw beyond display
The withering blossom of your lovely self?

For you had living still to do before
You slipped away onto an alien plain.
I like to think that you're at peace out there
Conversing on the spiritual life of whales.

Grieving

1 Seaview Terrace

The house is a storybook, its pages walls
From the drawers spill endless photographs
She lingers by the window, light drowns
Her eyes, a hammock where they tumbled
Long ago, lies in the winter grass.
From the curtains she shakes all her names for him
Night grows on the ceiling, shapes change
Her sad hands linger on the piano keys
She touches the blanket where his hands were laid
At midnight she'll lie down in the garden
Of their bed, the warmth his side fades
Like summer heat. Yet still she sees outside
The counterpane one blue pyjama'd leg
While through the wardrobe door his old clothes
Gleam like ghosts. She turns her face to the wall.

St Joseph's Home

I'm in a different place, my chair
Is not the same, wrong smell, wrong stains
Yesterday, tomorrow or today
She came, will come, is coming to me
I miss the paraphernalia of her rooms
Her breezy busyness, her scolds
My mind is now a cupboard of old days
The cold of school, wet football fields
My brother's misdemeanours. I peached on him
Would do it still. My children, three
Or is it four, all good to me. But chocolate bars
And sweetened tea my children now. And she –
Is it today, tomorrow, yesterday, she'll come to me.

The Sadness of the Dead

Beside him she, his dearie, all bemused,
Through whose eyes streams music,
Tinkling sounds she's kneading with long fingers.

I rest by them to wait, unsure for whom.
Then the One is among us,
Wondrous afterglow.

Too soon, he whispers, drawing me aside,
In the press of hand on shoulder
A promise of return.

Desolate, I leave that circle of the dead,
All dithery with bliss, their feet deep
In fields of marigold, all dithery with bliss.

Dodo and I

It started with her weekly call.

'Are you alright for Wednesday, Minnie?'

'I can't see why not, Dodo.'

'See you then. Up at the Dargle.'

Or, she might have said 'at Daly's'. All the same to me. As long as we got out. Every week she phoned. We'd meet, either at the Windy Dargle in Dorset Street, or at Daly's opposite. Daly's was my favourite though. I didn't like the Dargle.

'Not a bad old shagger, really', Dodo would say, settling down to her first drink. She was still detaching from her man, Danny. He was tough on her. Very possessive. Mine could be worse, I'd say, to help her along.

We'd each buy the other a drink, and one for ourselves, making two. Then later, one for the road, making three in all. Around eleven, home we'd go. As we left the pub, I'd wipe my mouth and pat my handbag, as if to say, 'No harm done'. Dodo would shrug and toss her heavy hair. Her lips would tighten a little and her marvellous eyes would harden. Dodo was thirty-eight. I wasn't far behind. Between us we had five children.

This night was different though. I felt it as we sat at our usual table near the bar. Dodo started looking around. The Dargle had been done over recently. The lights were bright, so the barmen could see into every corner. The pub was too slick now for much atmosphere but Dodo thought it was smarter than Daly's. I liked the Daly's smell of smoke and drink, and heated bodies, the arguments going on in dark corners. I saw Dodo's eyes roam to a man at a table across from us. Distract her, I thought.

'I've always wanted to ask you. Dodo, it's a strange name.'

'Me real name's Teresa', said Dodo, without explanation, and still looking away.

'It was my grandfather called me Minnie', I offered, just to keep the chat going. '"Her name's Mary", my mother would say.'

'Lookat, I don't want to know about your mother, or your shaggin' grandfather', said Dodo, 'me mind's on other business. Tonight I feel like suspending disbelief and believing I'm a very desirable person.'

'Suspending disbelief." Where did you get that one?'

'There was a fella on the radio. Talking about books and things. And suspending disbelief. Like while you're watching a film, or reading a book, you suspend your disbelief in what's happening. Do you follow?'

'I'm managing …'

Dodo uncrossed her lovely legs, crossed them again, gave one of her meaningful shrugs, and continued her theme.

'I guess them stars, Demi Moore and Michelle Pffeifer and them, have to believe they're dead beautiful before they can act the part. Yea?'

I nodded, adding, 'Which they are, of course'. She continued talking to me, but looking at the other table.

'So, like I said, tonight I feel like suspending disbelief and believing I'm very desirable ...'

'To whom, Do?'

'Don't be like that, you. Listen, do you see them fellas over there?'

I pretended I didn't.

'For God's sake, Min. The real goodlooker with the green eyes.'

'Jesus, Dodo, how can you see the colour of his eyes through this smoke?'

'Yeah, well they're green, I'm telling you.'

'Would you call that suspending disbelief ... or bending it?'

'Funny tonight, aren't you?'

'I'm just glad to get out, Dodo. Anything seems funny.'

'Listen, we'll have another', she said. 'I'll get them.'

She stood up from her seat with intent. Her decision to be desirable was taking over. She didn't have to work too hard, mind. She's always been gorgeous. Without looking directly at anyone, she walked up to the bar, spreading what I'd call a message of availability. There was a new sway to her walk as she eased between the tables. Her hair, usually dragged back with a hair band, fell onto her shoulders, black and glossy. She seemed to have a new bra on too, or else she was really pushing them out. And bright lipstick with matching nails. She reminded me of my cat after a two-hours' preen. 'What's got into her?,' I asked myself. Watching her, I caught her mood.

'Two brandies and lemonade', I heard her call to Tommy, the barman.

'Is it yourself?', he asked, as well he might.

She ignored him. Putting her red nails around the brandies and the bottles of lemonade, she shimmied – that was the word for it – shimmied her way back to our table, lowering herself onto her chair with lascivious grace. That was a word I'd read recently in an old copy of *Harper's Bazaar*.

'What film are you in, Dodo?', I said, conscious of the effect her performance was having on the assembled drinkers, mostly male.

She fixed me with a stare I'd recently seen. Yes, Kim Bassinger in last week's Screen 1 offering at The Virgin. We'd seen it together. Dodo and I are real movie buffs. What we don't see in afternoon cinema, we see on video.

'Minnie', she said. 'Him. Was he …?'

'Was he watching you? The whole pub was watching. What's come over you?'

'Desire', said Dodo, closing her eyes.

I sniffed, raising my glass, and stole a look at the fellow she was lining up. He was a stunner alright. And he had that sort of clout that would make you aware of him, even if you weren't looking. Dodo had been quick to sense it.

There's a side to Dodo that's wild. Her need for excitement, I suppose. She's repressed it in the last few years. There hasn't been much scope, you could say, with her fellow unemployed and home all day. He works a bit on the black. And Dodo goes out cleaning. Takes the kids with her to get them out of his way. They used to have grand times, herself and Danny. People looked at her, but they looked at Danny too. He had an air of confidence and expectation. He laughed a lot, loved Dodo, teased her. And spoilt her. Now he's jobless, there's not the money. And he's grown grumpy and resentful, with an explosive temper. He tells me he still believes there are good times ahead for himself and Dodo. He's frightened she'll lose hope. The temper's his only outlet. 'She always forgives me', he says. And I know she does. But if he caught her with a fellow!

Yet Danny doesn't mind her going out with me. I'm not what you'd call a raver! But I haven't forgotten the fight. Nor has anyone else around here. Except Dodo. At least that's the way it was beginning to look.

'I'm going to the Ladies', she said.

I noted the route. On the way back, as she passed his table, I was shocked to see her bend over the man and ruffle his hair. She said something to him. I saw him smile.

'What did you say to him, Dodo? You're a trollop.'

'"You remind me of me first fella, and he was lovely." That's what I said.'

Again, she lowered herself slowly onto the chair. And waited. Sure enough, over he came.

'Are you girls on your own?'

'Yes, and we're quite happy, thanks', says Dodo.

But I could feel her antenna twitch. And so could he. With the aplomb of a man on the loose, he pulled up a chair for himself, in the same movement beckoning the fellow he'd been sitting with to join us.

'This is Mick. I'm Ger. Yours is a …'

'Did we say?', I offered with sarcasm.

Quick as a flash, though, Dodo says, 'Two brandies and lemonade, thanks boys.'

After that, there was no holding her. She elevated those eyebrows, plumbed out the red lips, waved her hands in alternative come-hither and touch-me-not gestures that had your man in a flummox, and ready for favours.

As for his pal, he was about as conversational as a bus driver after a night shift. Anyway, anxious to play down Dodo's antics, I kept as far a distance from him as a small table with four people sitting knee to knee would allow. He and I just more or less sat and observed the little charade going on before us.

'Are you … you know …?' Ger's opener to Dodo.

'Am I free?'

'Well, I wouldn't want to be moving in on someone's space …'

'I can look after my own space, thanks.'

'Yeah? I can tell you're not the submissive sort!'

'Oh, I can be all sorts', she said archly.

He grinned. Dodo was quick to sense her advantage. But so was he.

'I'd say you're a grand little fecker, though.'

Her eyes opened slightly wider. I was shocked, real shocked. This man was a thug. But what about Dodo? If things were taking a different direction from the usual course of our Wednesday night out, was she not falling into her role like a woman with nothing to lose?

'Dodo, let's get out of here. You're going too …'

'If you don't mind, Min, I'll be in charge of me own brakes.'

Ger for Gerry, quick to sense my unease, laid his hands on Dodo's in a proprietorial gesture that left me right out in the cold. I turned to pal Mick.

'Does your friend always move so fast?'

'Does yours?', he asked.

I didn't answer but watched them edge nearer and nearer. After a few minutes of loaded chat, he suddenly took her face in one confident hand and kissed her full on the lips. Then continued talking. As if nothing had happened. After that, the chemistry between them was so electric even Mick the lad looked uncomfortable. Dodo's eyes grew black with static. She must have soaked herself in perfume. The heat of her arousal wafted not only over our table but I swear over the whole pub.

Ger called the barman over.

'What are you two talking about?' I whispered to Dodo. 'I'm telling him he's like Liam Neeson.'

'On with the disbelief, I suppose ...'

'Well, it's more than you could do with yours', she whispered, giggling.

'You're dead right', I said. 'He's too young to be Dracula.'

She let out a great laugh. And then her man, settling the drinks on the table, put his hand round Dodo's shoulders again, with the same 'she's for me' gesture. 'Not if Danny comes in', I thought.

Dodo's eyes danced with the tension. Not mine though. Not Tommy the barman's.

It was he who had broken up that fight Danny had started a few months back. The man had to be hospitalised. Danny was lucky not to be prosecuted. His friends in the pub intervened, saying the man had provoked him.

Now I'm not Dodo's keeper, but it was plain to me I had to do something. I knew, or thought I knew, Dodo was on for adventure only as long as it was curtailed by the pub. If she were seen to leave with a man, it would get around by more than one embroidered account. Not that you could add much embroidery to her present star performance. She was already in danger, I thought, because I sensed a bit of a hush around us. Local pubs are all eyes and ears.

To give myself time to think, I went to the Ladies. The window was one of those you can see out of but not into. It looks out on the lane at the side of the pub, parallel to but not into the street that fronts it. As I'm thinking by the basins, who do I see but Danny walking past on his way to the front. 'My God', I thought, 'Dodo is too dressed up. That's it. I've got to get her out of here.' I charged back to our table, which was out of sight of the door.

'Dodo', I hissed, grabbing her, 'Danny. He's coming in. I saw him from the window.'

She was out of her seat in a flash. We stumbled into Tommy the barman.

'Tommy, Tommy', I said. 'It's Danny. He's coming in. I saw him from the window.'

Tommy had been observing the scene from behind the bar. Tommy knew Danny. Tommy also had an eye for Dodo. 'Jesus', he said, 'out the back, girls.'

He opened up the back door with a great clatter of bolts and a chain that clanged against the wood. 'Don't worry, girls, I'll keep him talking', he whispered after us, as we ran through the slummy yard. Dodo fell over a bin, cut her leg. I dragged her onto the street.

'We're getting a taxi', I said, trying to flag one down. Unheard of for us. But we had to get home, very fast. Dodo was crying, and cursing Danny at the same time.

I put my arm around her. 'He smelled a rat, Dodo', I said. 'You looked too good.'

'I don't want to go home, Mini. He's no fun any more. He keeps me down. I'm still young, amn't I?'

'Young and beautiful, Dodo. Always.'

She was shaking. Her leg was bleeding. I held her hand. A taxi drew up. I bundled her in. 'The flats', I said. We were only going two streets. She was still crying. In the back of the cab I put my arm around her. And cried too. For her. With her. She was too beautiful.

'He's not that bad a man, Dodo. You know that. He has a temper. But he loves you. He'd never desert you. Didn't you have your bit of suspended disbelief anyway, love?'

The taxi stopped. Danny was standing on the pavement. He'd been quicker than us. We got out, slowly. I paid. Dodo was deathly pale.

I turned to Danny.

'She hurt her leg. Couldn't walk home. Did Tommy tell you?'

'Yes.'

Danny gave me a funny look before grabbing Dodo's arm.

'Come in home, Teresa', he said. 'I'll look after you.'

★

The Angel of Mons

(August 18th, 1914)

The wings are magnificent
The usual shape
The feet are obscured by flame
As if they are led through a chamber of light
Men walk off the battlefield
Unscathed

How does the soldier know
Who has only words to tell
The word he thinks of is 'Angel'
Because this is like nothing he's known
Instead of the smell of death
He smells spring and flowers
Whatever is his delight

Maybe it isn't a real angel
But while it hangs there
The dying is sweet and in any case
Stupefied by the light
The enemy holds back
Allows the besieged to retreat
Who hearing no shells
Weep among themselves
For their deliverance

Stillness settles
The trenches are filled with light
Strangers walk among the wounded
Tend them with shining hands
It is also related how a dirge was heard
From absent throats
The ghosts of the dead
Lamenting their pitiful state

And what of the other side
Whose guns are silent
As if they had gone off to tea
Failing to carry out orders
Because – they say –
Their horses have fled like the wind
Refusing to turn into that light

All this evidence it may be said
Comes through channels
Entitled to respect

The Misjudgement of Paris

When Helen left her man and went to Paris
She took along the face of Menelaus
Kindly, humourous, and missing her in Sparta.

Paris, the darling boy of Aphrodite
Vain and pouty, and a wimp in warfare
Philoctetes saw him off but not before

Those topless towers fell. Meanwhile, knowing
Where her bread was buttered, Helen climbed
Back on to the lap of Menelaus

And brushed her shiny hair across his eyes
He, good man that he was, spoiled her like a child
Helen grew plump and rosy eyed, no doxy she,

But sometimes when she thought of Paris
And that doting goddess Aphrodite who
Procured for her the golden boy, she sighed.

Theseus and Ariadne

Battle hot, he finds her in
The cool interior of Knossos,
Loves the entreaty in her eyes,
Slowly unwinds her tapestry of smiles
Half sighs, blushings, little wiles
Leading him into intimacies.

Daedalus had loved her clever eyes,
Built her a dancing palace, taught her artifice
In a clew of thread. Dionysius, the gentle,
The decadent, had wooed her with
The Corona Borealis given him by Amphitrite.
Now Theseus listens to her song:

'Be my deliverer, Theseus. Be the spider
To my silver thread.' Into the dark web
Of the Labyrinth she slides, her starry crown
Lighting his way, leaving him all the length
Of that long amorous journey to unwind
Exalted by her love game, he slays the Minotaur,

Takes her in his white-sailed ship to Dia.
Lying in the half-light of that pleasure isle
He strokes her milky limbs, uncoils her labyrinthine
Hair. But in the morning's sun he sees the flaw.
In place of a pretty foot, a cloven claw.
He leaves her like a folded flower on Dia's shore.

Dido and Aeneas

High on the poop deck sly Aeneas dozed
Dreaming of Troy and a favourable west wind
And as the dawn crept up he cast the ropes
That bound him to his Carthaginian queen.
Betrayed and shamed, Dido, from her tower
Made out the furl of his sails' cut and run
Across the water ran her screams: Aeneas, thief,

I salvaged you as flotsam on my shore
Under the dripping stars you came and now
You sneak away by dawn's back door. I hate
Your Trojan towers, your father king.
I am a queen, not yours to cast aside
Before our marriage bed has lost its heat.
And so her scalding tongue ran on until
Her maids came running to console her
But still she cried: He's left me without child
By whom to know him. Sisters, build a pyre,
Lay on it his clothes, all the sweet intimacies
He left by our bed. I loved him while the Fates
And God allowed. Leave me to watch them blaze.

When the women left, she climbed onto that fire
And drew the sword she'd hidden in her robes
Then plunged right down on it. But before she died
She drew across her face the veil of wild
Acanthus flowers Aeneas had given her
In their love throes. And from that bitter gift
A thousand gauzy stars rose up to pierce
The blackened sky above his scuttling ships.

Antigone

Creeping out from Argos she tracks by starlight
The path of her bad boy brother, with the wail
Of a lost bird uses hands and nails to claw
The soil of his grave, when Creon's henchmen
Find her, knows that like the last bright star,
She will disappear before morning glows.

Walled in stone, she allows herself an hour
For dreaming, of spring in Thebes, wildflowers
Barbarous on the hills, her lover in the fields,
Air tumbling between her arms, her thighs,
Her smallest bones. A soft wind stirs
Her labyrinthine hair. There is no light.

She spits the darkness out of her mouth,
And with a cry of the thing done, her soul
Moves into the space left by that sentinel star
To lamplight all the nights when a sister
Creeps along the Falls Road to lay a coat
Over the riven body of her brother.

The Return of Odysseus to Ithaca

When he limped home smelling of the world, stood under
The great gate of the courtyard, shreds of vigour
In the wiry hair, the ageing limbs still sinewed
She saw him from her window, knew she had acted right
But hard with anger for the loveless wait, withdrew
Into the shadows of her room, for three days cried
To her unborn sons, counted twenty notches
On the olive post he'd hewn and whittled for their bed
Heard his bellowed rage from the old banquet hall
Swagger of the warrior his gander up, thud of cross-bolt
Cudgelled skulls, blood on the tapestries, and when
His anger spent, he leaned exhausted by the fireplace
She fixed her face and hair, came down to him, cradled
His fading manhood and drew the sting of their lost years.

The Traveller

He stood by the wall, a bit down the road from the house, watching. Nobody came in or out. The house itself was not important. It could be any of the many he stopped at for a cup of tea or some company, leaving behind a bit of luck maybe, as he passed in and out. In any event, the houses were never the same. The day was dying quietly, smothered by the rising dark. A flock of starlings rose out of nowhere and disappeared behind the trees back of the house. There was a light wind blowing a paper cup along the road. When he was tired of watching, he approached the house and rang the bell.

The door opened. A woman, about his own age, looked at him intently.

'Yes?'

'I'm looking for the man of the house, a bit of work for tomorrow, perhaps?'

In one breath she gave him three answers.

'My husband's dead. He's just died. He died tonight.'

'Well I'm sorry for your trouble … I won't disturb you.'

'I'm glad. He gave me nothing.'

'Nothing? That's a hard thing to say about your husband.'

'He gave me no childer.'

Her eyes were angry, full of thwarting. He sensed a pleading in her hands, in the lean of her body. Did she want something from him? He lingered uneasily.

'Is he still in the house?'

'Yes. The doctor came. Then a nurse to lay him out. They'll be back in the morning to take him to the church.'

'You have a nice wee house, anyway', he said lamely.

'A nice house in the middle of nowhere. He needed a housekeeper, so he did. He wasn't up to anything else.'

'Did you perhaps want just that?'

'I was desperate.'

'For what?'

'For a babby.'

She looked at him again, her eyes running all over him.

'How old are ye?' she asked.

'Old enough', he said, evasively.

'Never mind', she said, and she looked away.

'Listen. You're a foolish woman. What do you know of me?'

She turned her eyes away in misery. 'Go off so', she said, slamming the door.

★

He stayed for a while on the doorstep. The last of the light picked up the paper cup caught in the fence. After a while he sat down, resting his backside on the doorstep. It wasn't good, the man just dead, lying in the house. And the woman didn't attract him. But he read her alright and felt drawn to her predicament. The husband had only this day died … there was just time. She wanted a child but she wanted it respectable or there would be no living for her in these parts. He'd seen women like her, servants all they were needed for, looking after some old fellow fearful of his last years. And the loneliness of their lives, on a small farm in the middle of nowhere. He left me nothing, she'd said. No child to dawdle on her plump knees, bury her face in its soft pink body.

He rang on the door again. 'If you'd ask me in for a while …'

She jerked her head in the direction of the warm hall. Giving a quick look up and down the road, she closed the door behind him, led him into the kitchen. For a moment, he felt panic. It was a room full of comforting smells, hung bacon, turf smoulder, carbolic soap or some disinfectant, whatever it was, he supposed, you washed people down with before you laid them out. Soiled bed linen was heaped in a corner. A cat stretched out by the fire. She shoved it out of the way with her foot and bent down to stoke up the fire, making time, he thought, for him to get used to the room, and to her.

'Will ye eat?', she said, but before he could answer, afraid he'd have her wasting her time, she took glasses from a cupboard, and a bottle of whiskey, pouring a large one for him, a small for herself.

He watched her, curious to know how she would approach him, how she'd manage the situation, now she had got him inside the house. He wondered but didn't ask about the husband, or where he was laid out. He presumed no one would be back tonight, though he didn't know. She seemed so isolated, not likely to have friends.

Her movements as she took down the glasses from the cupboard were lithe and confident. She's hardly forty, he thought. Under the black hair, the skin was taut, the cheek flushed. He watched the firelight play on the stocky arms as she leaned her palms on the table so as to swing round and sit with him. He wanted her to get up and move around again so he could study her body. But he bent over his glass, feeling her eyes on him. With a sudden lunge, she grabbed his arm.

'You know what I want.' He knew alright, but wasn't sure yet would he oblige her. He stalled.

'Give me a while now. Let me get a few drinks down.'

'Ye won't be able.'

'I'll be able. Just sit for a while, will you? Is everything done with the corpse? Will anyone be coming back this night?'

'There'll be no-one now till morning. I don't know many around here. He kept himself to himself.'

'How did it happen?'

'Why are ye bothering about him? He had a heart attack of a sudden, I suppose. He died in a few minutes. I'm glad he's dead, the useless old codger. For all the filthy talk on him, he couldn't do it. "I'll give you this, I'll give you that." A babby, a babby, that's all I wanted, more than me own life. I put up with his sour breath, his fumblings. He gave me nothing. I curse him, so I do.' Her anger shook the table.

He tossed the whiskey back, held his glass out for another. The bottle rattled against his glass as she filled him up again.

'Drink some yourself. It will help you to relax.'

'I don't need …'

'Take it.'

When she'd finished the glass, he stood up. Taking her by the elbow he turned her towards him, put his hand on her breast. She shrugged off the hand on her elbow. So he held her hair at the neck, where it was thickest, drawing her head back. But she wanted no formalities. She was impatient, crude, tearing at his trousers before he had them half down, tearing at her own clothes, pulling him down on top of her on the hard floor. It was over before the cat had time to get out of the way, leaving both of them breathless. Her frenzy, and the whiskey, had excited him so that he came quickly.

He was no sooner done than she was pushing him off her, and up fumbling with the bottle to fill his glass, not looking at him. He did himself up, smoothing his hair, feeling a long shudder ran through him from his brush with the woman's will.

'How do you know it will work?', he asked, somehow uncertain of the consequence of their clumsy coupling.

'It's the right time, so it is', she said with unexpected shyness.

'Where is the deceased anyway?'

'In the room above.'

'Take me up.'

She had relaxed, as calm now as she had been angry a while back. She mounted the stairs before him, her body casting shadows on the wall from the dim house light. The room was lit by two candles. He walked to the bed where the candles at each end threw flickers over the corpse. A man of about seventy lay with his hands crossed on his chest, a rosary wound around them. The man's head was bound to keep the mouth shut. A large man, overweight, flabby, the shirt he'd been laid out in taut across his chest and stomach.

The traveller studied the corpse for a few minutes. It seemed to have a good colour, none of the blueness about the mouth, the waxen skin of a dead man. A fearful thought passed over him. From a table, he took a hand mirror, held it against the mouth. It misted.

Jesus God! What had she said? The doctor who had been, could he have made a mistake? He had, there was no doubt. Maybe the man's heart had stopped momentarily. And the nurse? She would have done what she was told, and with the man in a coma and the doctor's word, would she notice? The doctor must be called in again. How had he got himself into this?

He crossed to the door, hesitated, crossed back, held the mirror again to the man's mouth. Mist. What if the man was buried alive? Sure his life was all but gone anyway. And if he recovered? And in time discovered the woman was pregnant? He'd throw her out for sure. But what had it all to do with him? He'd made his choice. A life on the roads, not in a house with small rooms, closed windows, and someone who wouldn't mean to nag but be driven to it by his solitary nature. No reason why he should do more to help this woman.

He put his head on the man's chest. Unsure could he hear the heart, he held the wrist. No beat from the pulse. He continued to stand in the near-dark, holding an uneasy vigil with the yellow candles.

'Why are ye stayin' so long there?'

Her voice was a thunderbolt from the door. He swung around to face her.

'Your husband. He's not dead. I'm telling you now. And I'm leaving. It is up to you to do what you must.'

'What are ye talking about? Get out of here, ye liar. Get out before I call the police.'

She flew at him, her fists raised. He caught hold of them.

'Listen woman, hold that mirror to his mouth. Do you see? It's misting. The man is alive. In a coma, that's all.'

She sank to the floor, her head in her hands, rocking herself to and fro. Her distress cut into him, weakening his urge to get away. The room seemed to grow darker. He was caught in her frenzy, impaled on the fury of her will. Despite himself, he felt a compulsion to draw her up.

'Listen. Don't fret now. He can't take the child from you, if it's a child that's there. He can put you out of the house but in law you are his wife. When he dies, what's his is yours. He'll die soon anyway. Go away, if you wish, when your time is near, when you start to show. But you have to do the right thing now. Call the doctor in again. I'm going to leave. I've done what I can for you.'

He made for the door, leaving his words to hang limp in the air. She struggled to her feet, ran after him.

'You're leaving me like this?'

He stopped. She stood beside him. Again, he felt the strength of her need, felt the fine life in her begging to be passed on. Wasn't the old man's life all but over? He took a pillow from under the comatose head. There was no struggle. The quiet of death filled the room. When he took the pillow away, held the mirror to the lips, the glass was clear. He turned to face her.

'Good luck to you now', he said. And left the house.

★

Vermeer's Milkmaid

Fecund as Demeter
She pours her milky flow
Into the waiting bowl

Fulfilling the intent of her face
And steadying arms
Her solid form

Bent solicitously
To the toil
Of serving her master

Who allows no
Extraneous
Shape or form

To intrude
On his report
Of sacred routine

Such order
Does he put
On his young maid

Deifying her
Her produce
And her task.

Looking into Corot's *'Ville d'Avray'*

Corot is my winter laureate
draws me to the Gallery to see
a simple scene of river field and tree
ether white beneath a sluggard sky

A figure turning from the riverbank
to look at me and overall the drift
of an uncanny mist so though I know
where trees field and riverbank should be

Each is wraithlike silvered vapourised
as if this were the last landscape
the gods had visited in stealth
on which to lay a cloth of shadeless light

And now the riverbank recedes
and trees give up their skeletal identity
while the girl figure has already crossed
the river and is waiting for me.

Bonnard's Waterwoman

This supine nude I stare on
Myself in bath. Bonnard
Wants to paint me, legs
Of Dordogne green
Asymmetric hips all still

Go away, Bonnard,
I'm no fish woman
To be stabbed in strict form
I'll paint myself
Squidge fingers in the soap
To join up stipple moles
Trace the in-between
And undulating
Inlet of the legs
Bays of the underarm

And my waterlily breasts
With what brushstroke will I cup
Their pink convex, caress
That arch of rhomboid thigh
Light moving in the water
This is no still life

See how the rounded plane
Of my blue belly
Is now dappled
Now doused in yellow
From the swinging bulb
That catching my thicket
Glints the way
To the rosemadder pool.

Now I see me in reverse
My underwater shade
As I let the water out
One of me will slip away
Leaving behind
A beryl green
Soul rim
For you, Mr Bonnard.

Painting Seamus Heaney

Here is the task, old man
Note the distance
between man and mask

Mould well the dome of the head
Inscrutable rock that puts clout
on the words to be read

Score well the line between soul and eye
Let light stream in
like underwater images of sky

Hold out for definition.
Be exact with the pitch of intellect
and scrutinise the gift

But who is this sitter you call
as open as the dawn
solid as the rocks of Donegal?

The Irish poet. And yourself?
Rembrandt, of course.
None other.

Lazarus To His Sisters

In your house at Bethany forbidden to love Him
I had looked at Him with lascivious eyes
the toss and furl of magenta hair
the carnal mouth, the lissom thighs

Through the flame of morning He'd hauled me
trailing my linen, my soul's gossamer.
For an instant I lingered, bathed in the miracle
as He unwrapped my face, opened my eyes

Whilst Mary and Martha stood weeping
imploring intercedance from the Father
who had turned away to allow the Sacrifice.
Afterwards we lingered, fearful, suspicious

Clinging together to blot out fear
as we lowered him into the poor man's pit
and gentling the warm earth around him
slinked away into our awesome future

The Stag

'Dirt', she cried, 'dirt, dirt', as she rubbed the mud from her face, from her legs, from her hands. The same word, over and over, as she got to her feet and ran down the road, falling, getting up, falling again, whimpering it outside the house, her palm hard on the doorbell, her forehead on the cool of the glass panel.

It was a while before he came to the door. She stood crumpled under the light, her face smeared and black, her clothes opened, torn. Fearing what had happened, he was careful not to show alarm. He drew her gently inside the house and led her to the bathroom. He had been under the shower. The water was still running. He undressed her carefully, standing her under the soothing water for a long time, drying her gently, all the while murmuring, 'Don't think about it, don't think …', as he led her to her bed. 'Don't think about it'.

Sitting beside her, he continued to calm her until she stopped her mouthing of the same word, unclenched her hands, and fell asleep. He stayed by her bed for a long time, studying her in the half-dark. In sleep, her face was shadowed by emotion. Her daytime face, the face she turned to him, was always unshadowed and cold. 'Let me in', he'd whisper, craving closeness like a child. But she gave him no warmth. He could not touch her, nor could he endure her rejection.

After some time he slipped into bed beside her, lying on his back exactly as was she, his hands clenched outside the sheet. He thought of the white tablecloth she laid between them when they ate together, and which she shook into the garden immediately after their meal to remove the crumbs.

She slept till late morning. When she got up, she washed for a long time before coming downstairs. He sat her beside him, asked for a description of her ordeal. She told him little, only that she had been walking by the river. It was very dark. There was no moon. An animal-like form had loped up behind her, brought her down on the riverbank. A fine point of silver gleamed against her throat, warning her, 'Don't scream'. There was no voice. The only sound breaking the silence was the hiss of what she called 'a violent horrible thing'.

Over the weeks that followed, she showed no signs of being disturbed. Their life continued as before. But he noticed that she began to wear unusual jewellery, and none that he had given her. The first piece was a silver watch, its face exquisitely worked with jewels. She removed it from her wrist each night and laid it down on a bedside table, quite unhidden, as if it were something she had owned all her life. He asked no questions.

The next piece he noticed was a pendant, embossed with tiny points of colour. The gleam of this delicate ornament, in the half dark in which she sat by the window, caught his eye. He followed its circle around the silk of her neck. She felt his scrutiny and turned to look at him with a face that held no explanation.

More pieces appeared. He saw on the third finger of her left hand, from which her wedding ring had been removed, a hammered silver ring with a stone of zaffer, the colour of her eyes. Some days later, a brooch in the shape of a moth, jewel-winged, appeared pinned above her left breast. These pieces were set out nightly beside the silver watch.

'She is transforming herself into a moon goddess', he thought, as he watched the moonlight stroke her sleeping face. He thought of Diana, the chaste huntress. Had not she too bedecked herself in silver when Actaeon followed her in the chase and saw her naked beside the stream? He chose to analyse her actions through myth rather than presume she was thieving to alleviate some distress.

Still he asked no questions. The thefts, if they were such, were numerous. All of the pieces were valuable. Each day he put them away in her drawer but each evening she again laid them out, arranging them on her bedside table so they caught the waning light. He himself became somewhat obsessed by them, as if they were plucked from deep within her, as if she were displaying her cold soul to him, untouchable, elusive, an exotic decoration of the mask.

As he lay beside her, her coldness burned into him, generating an excitement he could hardly bear. Asleep, he floated as on an icy lake, her lunar beauty burning above him, a wraith-like flame beyond his reach. These sensations remained with him each day so that he rushed home to be drawn again into her sorcery.

Then, as if she had completed her collection, no more new pieces appeared. Now he stopped putting the pieces away. Yet she herself covered them during the day with a cloth, removing the cloth at night as if the table was indeed an altar to the moon. It was as if she was elevating herself onto a nocturnal plane. In his complicity, he felt she had anointed him as her priest, celibate and untouched.

The night the policewoman called she was alone. Telling him of the questioning when he came in, she said the young woman was tenacious, probing her for information, questioning how often she left the house, what stores she patronised, recent purchases, other details. But he sensed the visit had agitated her, for he later found her pacing up and down the room, stopping to look out into the garden, drawing the curtains over, drawing them back again. He thought he again saw her lips forming the word 'dirt'. She went upstairs and came down a little later, her jewels on her neck, her hands, her breasts. Her long hair was combed loose, and her eyes were more distant and cold than he had ever seen them.

'I am going to walk by the river', she said.

He didn't try to stop her but when she had gone, he followed her at a distance. She stood for a long time looking into the river. The moon lit up her bright hair, threw her shadow on the bank. He watched as she walked slowly down to the water's edge. She stood for a long time with her arms outstretched, then took some steps into the water and slowly laid herself down on its swollen surface. He did not call to her, or move to pull her back. Watching her, he drew from his pocket a silver knife, the blade of which he stroked and stroked as her body, soused with slime and weed, sank under the black water.

He continued to stroke the knife, drawing his hands along the fine edge, until the water had settled. Slowly, he replaced it in his pocket, and set off for home. Rounding the corner of the road, he broke into the loping gait of a stag.

*

Mirage

When the boy appeared out there
Pale as the haze of noon,
All wrapped in shimmering linen,
His arms in flames, his eyes
Full of his own being,

It was a visitation unheralded
That found me drowsy under
Summer trees, the air so bright,
The boy so stilled, so shined
Wearing his ineffable peace.

Yet even as I fathomed him
His fading linen snooked
On the wind, the sun withdrew,
The earth shook itself and I was left
With rounded eyes

To shiver in the grass,
Feel the waning day,
See the stilly hole of light
In the shaded tree
Where a god had been.

The Witching Hour

Now comes that witching hour when night's blue glow
Glides languidly towards dawn, in whose sly rise
Your head's dark gloss finds form. Yet still I know
That when the soul is still, the day's eyes closed,

How softly ghosts can glow and though I sigh
For you, I stay my hand, unwilling to disturb
Your dreams lest they be of me. For come daylight
Old enmity may wake, our backs be turned,

And love's reality still scorned. But yet
Upon those tight shut eyes, that tight shut mouth,
My need of you directs my tongue to light
And damn the animosity that shuts me out.

You stir. I weep. Such is the end to sleep.
Dawn sees us bound and wound, each to each.

Night Air

(for Dermot)

I love your walking in on me each night,
Not the usual wisp and tatter of the
Undressed ghost but resolute and bright
In your own clothes, outstretched hands saying

It is I. But come and see, outside this room
The salvias still bloom, the window breathes
Warm air through rattan slats, in the French door
Shines the bronze haze of the chrysanthemums.

Strange, you are not reflected there. Needing
No space, you are in me. Come, sit down,
Your glass is filled. I thought my heart tomb dark
But love is rogue and it is I who call you.

Asphodel

All night I search for faces I have lost
Then seem to die. And find them elsewhere
In a breathless circle of each other

Clothy as air,
Cooing the noises of the dead
Whether to be again.

There sits that man I loved.
I kiss his mouth. *Come here* he sighs,
Turning on me his brimming eyes

And there my learned father, round whose head
A swarm of hieroglyphics. *You talk no more?*
There is no more, he says.

The Wood Pigeon

A tree bends over you like Yeats' old thorn,
How desolate the day, your place in it.
I push the graveyard gate, walk slowly through
The gloomy avenues of stone and fern.

I buried you in the wrong place, the wind
Is softer from the west than from the east;
Your feet should face the sea like any Celt.
But I'll do what I can to clear your space,

Brush off the sodden leaves, replace the lead
Of letters fallen off your name, our name.
And I'll not ask what of you perished first
Yet hear the truth, that all is gathered up

In human love. I've left you some flowers.
Is it the rain or you who flays my face,
Or wind dements my hair? I turn to leave.
A wood pigeon breaks from the trees,

A whirr soft as a ghost. I listen to it
As it comes and goes, comes and goes.

Desecration

On the verge of the macabre you lie
In the make-over parlour of the Dead,
Your hands, your shining hair lightless
Like the black box of your bed, your leaden
Eyes vacant as a glass without a face.
That is not you, I cry, *that's a grotesque.*

See how the spirit's lack has reduced
Your darkling beauty to an unlit coal.
Again I cry: *My love is elsewhere. He racks
My soul.* I kneel to kiss your icy effigy,
Scream at the hovering funeral man:
You've desecrated him. He cannot rest.

The Intruder

It was when he was crossing his own kitchen that the foreign woman looked at him. She looked at him in the face. No smile, no greeting, nor did she say hello. He noticed her eyes. They were hard and luminous. Like stones after rain, he thought. She had come to live in the cottage up the road. His wife, partly from curiosity, partly from neighbourliness, had told the woman to drop in on some Tuesday afternoon. The other women along the road would be there, she said.

There were five of them in the room, all chattering and hooting like a pack of birds. But she sat silent, a little apart. The women probably chattered more than usual because she made them feel uncomfortable. She seemed so self-contained, answering any questions put to her with short succinct answers that told them what they wanted to know and little else.

As he walked across the room, without any apparent movement she turned her body into his line of vision, looking him straight in the face. He felt himself blush and instead of joining the women for a brief chat, he walked through to the opposite door, closing it quietly behind him. In the passageway outside the door he paused, wondering why he had done that. And was annoyed with himself. But he shrugged his discomfort off and went back to work on his plot. He missed the cup of tea he had gone in for, and the talk of the women. But he didn't rejoin them, although the woman left soon after him. He watched her go back across the road, looking around her as she went through the gate to her own cottage.

The man saw her several times in the next few weeks. He'd raise his eyes to her and she would smile at him, a slight but positive smile that challenged him to smile back. After a few such encounters he found himself doing just that. She responded by asking him what she should do with her overgrown garden. It wasn't long before he was doing a bit of the heavier work for her. And not long after that again before he was sitting in her kitchen.

When she'd first suggested, after a stint of work for her, that he should take a cup of tea, he found himself blushing, as he had on his first encounter with her in his wife's kitchen. She, for her part, was off-hand with him, continuing with her tasks as he made awkward conversation. Then, quite unexpectedly, she sat down at the table, closer to him than she needed, and looked him directly in the face. 'We could be friends, you and I', she said. He felt an unease creep through him, and his face again reddened. Getting to his feet, he pushed the chair back awkwardly so it toppled over. 'Why should we not be?', he said. 'Aren't we neighbours?' She answered him with a slow smile, standing up to right the chair.

When he got home, his wife was bending over the old stove, trying to coax it into a flame. 'Let me do that', he said, feeling the need to be near to her. That night he slept with his arm thrown lightly across her back. And in the morning he kissed her as he awoke. She had looked demurely at him and smiled, as she had when she first met him, he thought. He'd kissed her because he had dreamed of the foreigner.

A handsome enough woman, he'd said to himself. In her forties, maybe. She had thick tawny hair, and a full mouth that had a way of sliding open to let out a few words. Her eyes were shrewd, her body heavy but sinuous. He found her strong sexual presence disturbing. He was, as she had intuited, almost virginal. He and his wife had been young when they married. Both came from the nearby town. They settled down together and were mutually content.

Though he disliked the woman somewhat, he found himself visiting her on some pretext or other almost every day, maybe to do with her garden, or the chickens she kept out the back, or the fact that her dog had strayed up the road and was a nuisance to motorists. The dog, he thought, got out too frequently, knowing in his heart it wasn't altogether the dog's fault.

Gradually, he gave in more and more to her ruses, often blushing at his own complicity, such as passing her door when he'd see her in her garden. He had a small farm at the back of his place, with livestock, and a large vegetable garden which took him to market once a week. She had, of course, observed his routine and worked in her own garden that day so he'd be sure to see her as he came and went.

It was on one of these days, when she'd called him in to look at something that needed fixing, that he took her in her own kitchen. She had been standing unnecessarily close to him so all his senses were alive to her. Sensing his unease, she had begun to taunt him for his sexual shyness. The excitement of that sudden coupling, his self-contempt surfacing in his rough handling of her, surprised him. 'You'll come again', she told him as he left her house. 'I will not', he said, crossing the road.

He didn't turn into his own house but continued to walk up the hill as far as the woods at the top. He often walked in these woods. They were an escape from the whirl of domesticity that was his young wife's world. Though he helped her in the house when he felt in the mood, or she seemed stressed. And she accepted his need for these solitary ramblings.

Now, as he entered the woods, the sun was going down. And it seemed as if the town below was on fire and the woods themselves wrought with flame. He sat down on the stump of a tree, felled before it could grow. He felt this half-grown tree beneath him to be himself, the persistent sapling springing up beside it the metamorphosis of that man who had just left the woman's house. The association pleased him and he mused on it for a long time. He didn't as yet feel any guilt. The woman's sexual boldness, and his audacity, fed his excitement. He became aware of a growing tumult in the sky. With the sinking of the sun, the birds were fighting for territory, and for mates. They were aggressively alive. They took what they wanted. As always, he was amazed by their energy and aggression. No manners. No manners at all, he said to himself, smiling at the realisation. And he knew he would see her again.

Indeed, he became devious and cunning in finding excuses to cross the road. His wife put his frequent visits down to neighbourliness. 'She is on her own', he'd say. 'She needs help with some of the heavy work.' Or, 'she's having trouble with her heating'; 'the water pressure is poor that side'; 'there's a broken window at the back'. He felt ashamed of his duplicity but was powerless to fight it. And so he found himself neglecting his tasks, taking long walks, his mind consciously avoiding the decision not to visit the woman. For his body was in turmoil and he was unable to control the imperative to be near her. Again, he taunted himself for his lack of will, his inadequacy.

But as soon as he was in her presence, he became that other man, the man who had delighted in the saplings he had seen in the woods.

The woman played her part too, saying, 'Good morning, dear', to his wife, who would be taking the children to school past the woman's door. Or she'd pop over for the loan of something, a kitchen tool, some change for the milkman, maybe collect some scraps for her dog. His young wife thought she was grand, loved her foreign idiom, was a little in awe of her. The woman would often bring her offerings, a cake, or some book she'd mentioned, a scarf or trinket maybe she'd claim to be tired of. 'That woman should mind her own business', he'd say, as these offerings were shown to him.

Yet whenever she met him with his wife, she amazed him by the way she ignored the younger woman and spoke only to him. 'The dog has something in his paw', she'd say, brazenly waiting for him to offer help. And the man was both uneasy at his wife's innocent connivance, and uneasy for playing what he knew in his heart to be a treacherous game. But he couldn't deny to himself that her brazenness aroused him. He was intrigued by her lack of emotion, though he felt no commitment to her. His visits might last only twenty minutes, at the most half an hour, so there was no suspicion on his wife's part, had it ever entered her head to suspect him. Nor, he thought, theirs being the only two houses on that bend of the road, were there likely to be observers of the blatant traffic. Yet, his wife's trust disturbed him, for he was both moved and belittled by it. 'She's making it easy for me', he thought, managing in his uneasiness to shift some blame on her.

But as the months went by, the man did grow progressively uneasy. He wasn't deceitful by nature, and the compulsion of his lovemaking with the woman was soon replaced by a sense of unworthiness. It wasn't shame. He didn't reproach himself for his infidelity. For he didn't associate that which he was experiencing across the road with the tenderness and love he felt for his wife. His unease was rather a revulsion for the neighbouring woman's blatant sexuality, and her disassociation of the sexual act with any tenderness or subtlety. She was cunning and dangerous, he came to recognise.

To his wife, she talked often of her friend in America, how the friend wrote to her every week. This was evidenced at the local Post Office by the regular deliveries from a James A. Clinton, and the wonder of the village would he be anything to the President himself. She showed his wife gifts the man purported to have sent her, small but expensive trinkets she would withdraw from a neat posted box, blushing, his wife said, like a young girl, as she displayed them.

It was the day on which he returned from market to find her leaning over his gate to talk to his wife, that he was overcome with anger, both for his own compliance, and for her brazen intrusion into his life. Slowly, he decided that he would make enquiries about her background, and her reason for settling in a quiet Irish village. Without harming the woman, he would compel her to leave.

For he recalled having several times seen an envelope on her table from the Federal Bureau of Investigation, Washington State. She had whipped it away when she saw it catch his eye. 'I'll phone the American Embassy', he thought. 'Ask them have they any record of a temporary female resident's passport in the name of Ms So and So.'

'Is she resident, or just travelling?', they enquired.

'Resident, as far as I know.'

'Reason for asking?'

'She's renting the house opposite my own, but she's been missing for a few days. Her windows are open, the dog hasn't been fed, and her lights are on.'

A pause on the line.

'Are you sure she's an American citizen?'

'Well, yes. I assume so. She gets mail from the States.'

'Please hold.'

After some minutes, the voice came back to him.

'We do not have a record of her passport. I'm afraid we can't help you. Perhaps you should contact the police.'

'I'll do that. Thanks for your help.'

When he had put down the phone, he felt ashamed of his action. But he had no compunction now but to invade her life as ruthlessly as she had invaded his. Repeating that journey of many months ago, when he had first left her house, he walked quickly up to the woods and sat by the same tree. He looked down on the town below him, and it was no longer bathed in light. Now the rain fell heavily through the young trees, and fell on him, washing him in its downpour, and washing away the muddied sludge under his feet that had once been a glorious carpet of leaves.

'She is destructive', he thought. 'She has sullied the town and I have sullied my love for my wife. I will be brutal with her, as she has been with me. I'll force her to leave.'

So he left the woods and walked back down the road and confronted her in her kitchen.

'You're not an American citizen, are you?'

Taken by surprise, she looked at him defiantly.

'And what is that to you, sonny?'

'I've been in touch with the US Embassy. They don't have a record of your passport.'

It had occurred to him, of course, that the name on the packages from the States might not be her real name. Now he knew. The information he'd had from the Embassy, or rather non-information, was no proof that she was, or was not, American. But it was proof she was travelling under a different name.

'Look', he said, 'I don't wish you any harm. But you don't belong here. You should go back to your own people.'

She remained silent for some minutes. 'Would you mind leaving?', she then said, in a voice that was totally controlled.

'I think it is you who should leave. You are in hiding, aren't you?'

'None of your god-dammed business. Your little wife won't be happy about your peccadilloes across the road, will she now?'

'That will be between myself and my wife. She will hear from me. But not from you, I fancy.'

She paused. And turned her back to him. After a long moment, she turned back to him.

'Okay', she said. 'We'll make a deal. You keep my secret and I'll keep yours.'

'I'm not making a deal with you. I simply want you to move from this village.'

She looked him full in the face, as she had first done in his kitchen. But now her eyes were cold with hate. And something else. Fear, he thought. His intuition had been right. She was running away.

In less than three days, she was ready to move out. She left behind her dog, her cheap furniture that had at first surprised him, her books – no name inscribed – a pair of broken shoes. These last, against his will, he found poignant.

Standing by her door as he helped her with the few items she was carrying, she turned to him to say:

'And have you not been pleased by me? Have I taught you nothing?'

He paused to consider her question. His eyes rested on the young woman across the road with the child on her hips. He watched her stoop among the flower beds, and straighten again, her face flushed and dreamy in the afternoon sun. And remembered that on the day the woman had come to live beside them, the cherry tree in her garden – for he thought of it as hers – was in its full blooming. But he had neglected to prune it before the present spring. Now, the blossom would not be so profuse. 'There's still time', he thought. 'There's still time.'

Turning to the woman, he bent forward and kissed her gently on the cheek.

'Yes', he said, 'you've taught me to love my wife.'

Then, half-walking, half-running, to the shed at the back of his house, he pulled out a shears and returned to the tree. With swift decisive strokes, he cut it back, the shame he felt for his neglect giving way to an optimism that with care it would return to richer loveliness.

★

About the Author

SHEILA O'HAGAN began writing in 1984 while studying at Birkbeck College, London University. In 1988 she won the Goldsmith Award for Poetry, and in 1990 returned to her native Dublin. In 1991 she won the Patrick Kavanagh Award and in 1992 the Hennessy/Sunday Tribune Award for New Irish Poet of the year. She has twice been awarded First Prize for Poetry at Listowel Writers' Week. She was the winner of the Strokestown International Prize for a single poem in 2000. Her short stories and poems have appeared in, among others, *The Adirondack Review*, *Atlanta Review*, *The Sunday Tribune*, *Syracuse Review* & *Working Papers in Irish Studies*. She has conducted literary workshops in Wormwood Scrubs Prison, UK, in Inter-City Schools, and for three terms in The Writers' Centre, Dublin. She was writer-in-residence for Kildare County Council from 1994 to 1996. In 1990 she conducted radio workshops for prisoners on 98FM. She was editor of the *Cork Literary Review* from 2005 to 2007. She also edited *Under Brigid's Cloak*, an anthology of Kildare writers, in 1994. Her previous collections, *The Peacock's Eye* (1992) and *The Troubled House* (1995), were both published by Salmon.